AUG 1 6 2005

W9-AUY-091

Bridgestone
BOOKS

World of Mammals

Polar Bears

by Erika L. Shores

Consultant:
Jaime R. Alvarado Bremer, PhD
Departments of Marine Biology and Wildlife and Fisheries Sciences
Texas A&M University
Galveston, Texas

Capstone
press

Mankato, Minnesota

Bridgestone Books are published by Capstone Press,
151 Good Counsel Drive, P.O. Box 669, Mankato, Minnesota 56002.
www.capstonepress.com

Library of Congress Cataloging-in-Publication Data
Shores, Erika L., 1976–
    Polar bears / by Erika L. Shores.
    p. cm.—(Bridgestone Books. World of mammals)
    Summary: "A brief introduction to polar bears, discussing their
characteristics, habitat, life cycle, and predators. Includes a range map,
life cycle illustration, and amazing facts"—Provided by publisher.
    Includes bibliographical references and index.
    ISBN 0-7368-4312-4 (hardcover)
    1. Polar bear—Juvenile literature. I. Title. II. Series: Bridgestone
Books. World of mammals.
QL737.C27S535 2006
599.786—dc22   2004028438

Editorial Credits

Shari Joffe, editor; Molly Nei, set designer; Biner Design, book designer; Patricia Rasch, illustrator;
    Kelly Garvin, photo researcher; Scott Thoms, photo editor

Photo Credits

Digital Vision Ltd./Jeremy Woodhouse, 1, 6
McDonald Wildlife Photography/Joe McDonald, 20
Minden Pictures/Flip Nicklin, 4; Foto Natura/Rinie Van Muers, 12;
   Michio Hoshino, 18; Mitsuaki Iwago, 16
Tom & Pat Leeson, cover, 10

1 2 3 4 5 6 10 09 08 07 06 05

Table of Contents

4

Polar Bears

Polar bears are <u>large bears</u> that make their homes on Arctic ice near water. Polar bears get their name because they live near the North Pole.

Polar bears are **mammals**. They have backbones and are **warm-blooded**. Like other bears, polar bears have thick fur to keep them warm in cold weather. The brown bear is the polar bear's closest relative.

◄ Polar bears are at home in the icy waters of the Arctic.

What Polar Bears Look Like

Polar bears have large bodies. Male polar bears weigh 700 to 1,700 pounds (317 to 771 kilograms). Female polar bears are smaller than males. They weigh between 330 and 550 pounds (150 and 250 kilograms). Polar bears walk on four strong legs. Their huge paws have sharp claws.

A polar bear's fur is not really white. It is made up of clear, hollow hairs. The hairs reflect light, making the fur look white. When dirty, a polar bear's fur looks yellow or brown.

◀ Polar bears are bulky. They have two layers of fur and a thick layer of fat called blubber.

Polar Bear Range Map

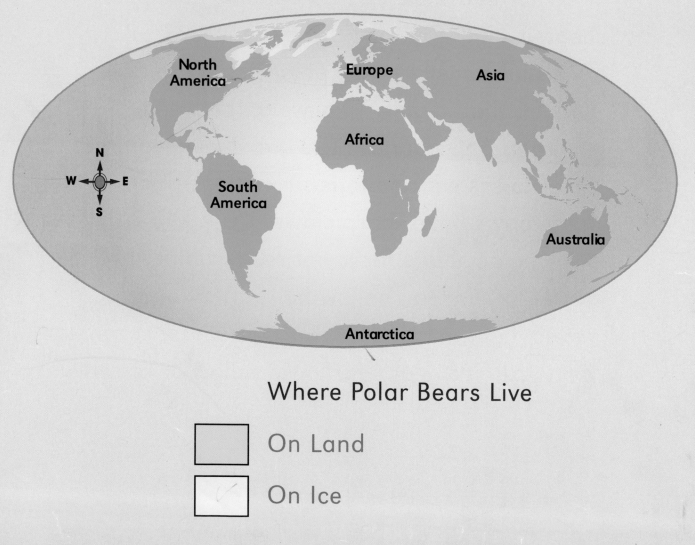

North America

Europe

Asia

Africa

South America

Australia

Antarctica

N
W — E
S

Where Polar Bears Live

On Land

On Ice

Polar Bears in the World

Polar bears live on sea ice near the Arctic Circle. They can be found in Arctic areas of Alaska, Canada, Russia, Greenland, and Norway. People living in these areas sometimes see polar bears. Polar bears enter towns when they can't find enough food to eat.

Polar Bear Habitats

A polar bear's **habitat** is the ice that floats near coasts and islands in the Arctic. Polar bears move onto land in the summer when the ice melts.

Polar bears spend much of their time in the water. They are often seen swimming far from land or ice.

In the fall, female polar bears dig snow dens. They crawl into an area of deep snow to keep warm. They stay in these dens all winter long.

◄ Polar bears live mainly on floating pieces of ice called floes.

What Polar Bears Eat

Polar bears are the largest **predators** on land. They hunt for the food they eat.

Polar bears feed mainly on seals. Seals swim under the ice and breathe through holes in the ice. A polar bear waits at a breathing hole to spot a seal. Then it grabs the seal with its sharp claws. Polar bears also sneak up on and attack seals resting on the ice.

When polar bears can't find seals, they hunt other animals. These animals may include birds, fish, and young walruses.

◀ A polar bear tears into a seal it has just caught.

The Life Cycle of a Polar Bear

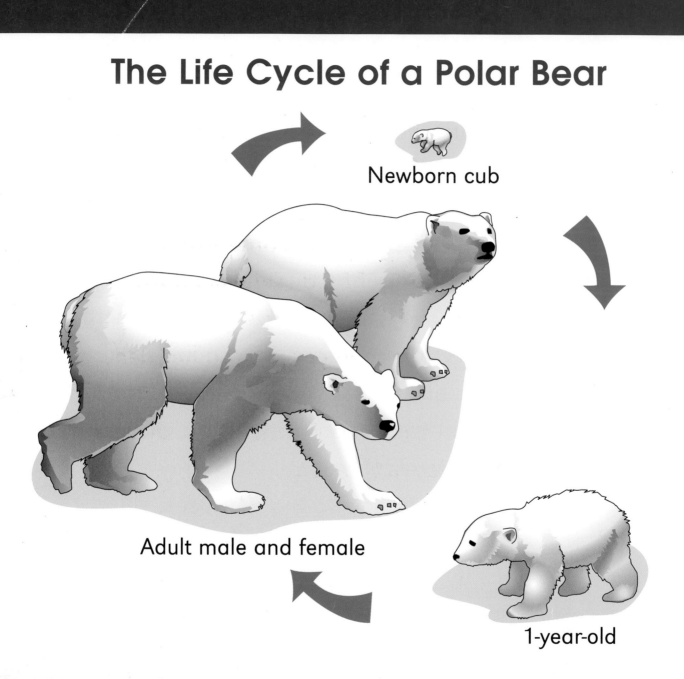

Newborn cub

1-year-old

Adult male and female

Producing Young

Polar bears live alone. Males and females come together only to **mate**.

Polar bears mate during April and May. After female polar bears become **pregnant**, they must eat a lot of food. They need to store fat on their bodies for the winter.

In October, a female crawls into her den. In December or January, she gives birth to one to three cubs. In the spring, the mother and her cubs leave the den.

Growing Up

Polar bear cubs are small at birth. They weigh a little more than 1 pound (0.4 kilograms). The cubs grow quickly as they drink their mother's milk. Six months later, they are ready to leave the den.

Cubs learn how to live on the ice. They run and play. They tumble over piles of snow. They slide down icy slopes. Cubs watch their mothers hunt seals. Soon, the cubs learn how to hunt on their own. Cubs stay with their mothers for about two years.

◄ Female polar bears and their cubs come out of their snow dens in the spring.

18

Dangers to Polar Bears

People are the only great danger to polar bears. Some native people in Arctic areas hunt polar bears for their meat and fur.

People also harm polar bear habitats. Companies drill for oil in Arctic areas. Drilling disturbs polar bears and their cubs. Oil spills **pollute** Arctic waters where polar bears live.

Some people help polar bears. They pass laws to limit hunting. Scientists study polar bears and their habitats. They are learning how to protect polar bears in the future.

◄ People bring changes to polar bear habitats.

Amazing Facts about Polar Bears

- Polar bears don't lick themselves clean. They roll in the snow or swim in the sea to clean blood and dirt from their fur.
- Polar bears have black skin under their fur.
- Polar bears can swim as fast as 4 miles (6.5 kilometers) per hour.
- Polar bears sometimes hunt for seals by swimming under the ice.
- About 25,000 polar bears roam the Arctic.

◄ A polar bear cleans its back by rubbing it against the ground.

Glossary

habitat (HAB-uh-tat)—the place and natural conditions where an animal lives

mammal (MAM-uhl)—a warm-blooded animal that has a backbone; female mammals feed milk to their young.

mate (MAYT)—to join together to produce young

pollute (puh-LOOT)—to make dirty

predator (PRED-uh-tur)—an animal that hunts other animals for food

pregnant (PREG-nuhnt)—having young growing inside one's body; female mammals may become pregnant after mating.

warm-blooded (warm-BLUHD-id)—having a body temperature that stays the same

Read More

Cotton, Jacqueline S. *Polar Bears.* Pull Ahead Books. Minneapolis: Lerner, 2004.

Hall, Eleanor J. *Polar Bears.* Nature's Predators. San Diego: KidHaven Press, 2002.

Internet Sites

FactHound offers a safe, fun way to find Internet sites related to this book. All of the sites on FactHound have been researched by our staff.

Here's how:
1. Visit *www.facthound.com*
2. Type in this special code **0736843124** for age-appropriate sites. Or enter a search word related to this book for a more general search.
3. Click on the **Fetch It** button.

FactHound will fetch the best sites for you!

Index